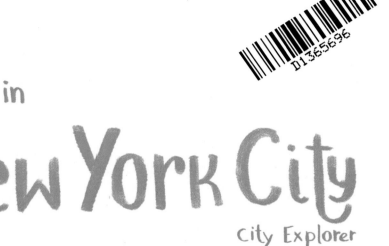

A Day in New York City

City Explorer

Read With You Center for Excellence in STEAM Education

Published by Read With You Publishing
Designed by Read With You Center for Language Research and Development
Read With You and associated logos are trademarks and/or registered trademarks of Read With You L.L.C.
ISBN-13:979-8-88618-134-0
First Edition April 2022
Printed in the United States of America.

Tim is a photojournalist. He takes exciting photos of places across the globe! But he isn't great at knowing where he is. Today he's enjoying the busiest city in the United States of America.

Rosa is a researcher who likes to work from her cozy home office. She finds all the facts that Tim needs. Rosa will help Tim appreciate the city's glamour and variety.

Good morning! So much to see and do today. Are you ready, Rosa? I'm going to climb this cool walkway.

Let's get going! That is Vessel. It was made to look like a beehive, and you can see across the river to the state of New Jersey from the top.

Wow, I want the same view of New York City. I'll head to the Empire State Building next. Why is it so famous?

The Empire State Building was the world's tallest building when it was finished in 1931. Four million people enjoy its views each year!

Incredible! The city's buildings looked huge while I was on the street, but they're far below me now. I feel so tall!

You should work there then! The building isn't just for tourists. It has company offices and a broadcasting antenna at its top.

Whew! I came all the way down and popped into the Grand Central Terminal.

Smart! Since 1913, this has been the bustling heart of the city. Every year, over 45 million people get on and off the train here.

I've seen this clock in movies! Now that I'm here in person, I see the information booth below. But why is the clock famous?

It's a popular place for people to meet because it's so easy to spot! The clock looks pretty in photos, too.

I checked the maps, and it was faster to walk to my next spot, the Rockefeller Center, because it is right here!

Yup! It is named after John D. Rockefeller, a super-rich New Yorker. Today, it's got art, stores, and even its own traditions.

That's a lot for one place! How big is the Rockefeller Center? And what traditions can a place have?

The center has nineteen buildings and tons of outdoor art. Its most famous tradition is the huge tree that is put up every Christmas!

I'll have to visit in December. I'm getting hungry. I've passed so many food trucks around here. Which do you recommend?

Try food from a halal truck! The gyros have meat, veggies, and a creamy yogurt sauce wrapped in pita bread... Now I'm hungry, too!

That was tasty! I'm glad I'm walking because the streets are always packed. Are these yellow cars all taxis?

Yes! NYC is always busy, so the taxi drivers use their deep knowledge of the city to zoom around! Good thing NYC has buses and trains, too.

I made it to Times Square! It feels like lights and sounds are coming from everywhere. There are people all around and screens above me.

It is noisy! Times Square is a top tourist spot with stores, restaurants, costumed performers, theaters, and souvenir shops.

I see so many signs for musicals and plays. Do people here love the theater?

You're near Broadway, which is famous for its musicals and plays. Watch a performance tonight. I'm sure it will be unforgettable!

I will, but I want nature now. All those bright lights were a little tiring. I'm so glad I found these trees.

You're not alone; many people need a break from the busy city. That's why Central Park was built back in the 1850s.

It is beautiful. And, I see art mixed in with the nature, like the cool architecture or this ballerina!

Many artists show off their work in Central Park. You can find artwork and souvenirs to buy, and everything from dancers to clowns!

Now that I've rested,
I need to fill my stomach again.
What special NYC food should
I have for dinner?

Pizza! There are 99-cent pizza
stores everywhere, but I would
go to a proper pizzeria for a
slice. You'll love it.

Whew, what a long and exciting day! I'm going to take a nap before I see a musical. Goodbye for now, New York!

Sleep well! You've certainly seen a lot today, Tim!

Learn

1. What do the buildings look like in New York City?

2. What was special about the Empire State Building in 1931?

3. Where can you go to see a musical in the city?

4. Where can you go to find nature in the city?

Imagine

1. Think about how many people live near you. How does your neighborhood compare to New York City's fast pace?

2. Which place in the city do you most want to see? Why?

3. Downtown NYC is easy to walk around because everything is close together! Where can you walk to from your house?

4. What kind of performer would you want to see in Central Park?

Act

Option 1

Research Grand Central Terminal. How has it changed since it was built? Where can you go from there? Write a paragraph about what you learned.

Option 2

Find a movie or music video with a scene from New York. Pause the screen when you see a place you recognize in the city. Draw a picture of the scene and put yourself in it!

Made in the USA
Columbia, SC
28 October 2022

70173193R00022